Twenty to Make

Steampunk Jewellery

Carolyn Schulz

Search Press

First published in Great Britain 2014

Search Press Limited
Wellwood, North Farm Road,
Tunbridge Wells, Kent TN2 3DR

Text copyright © Carolyn Schulz 2014

Photographs by Paul Bricknell
at Search Press Studios

Photographs and design copyright
© Search Press Ltd 2014

Print ISBN: 978-1-78221-012-2
Epub ISBN: 978-1-78126-205-4
Mobi ISBN: 978-1-78126-206-1
PDF ISBN: 978-1-78126-207-8

The publishers would like to thank Judith More
of Fil Rouge Press for providing props for
photography and styling.

Printed in China

Dedication
I dedicate this book to Chris and Steve at
Solid Oak who introduced me to making and
designing jewellery and to Chris Freedman at
Fire Mountain Gems and Beads for supporting so
many of my design projects over the years!

Contents

Introduction

My love affair with all things British, and the Victorian era in particular, started as a child when my mother used to read me *Bedtime Stories* by the English storyteller, Arthur Maxwell.

Given my attraction to Victoriana, it was not surprising that when Steampunk began to influence trends within jewellery, I quickly succumbed to its romantic representation of the period, which encompasses literature, fantasy, scientific theory, science-fiction, steam technology and discovery of all kinds.

Time plays an important part in Steampunk, where watch and clock parts such as gears and watch hands are often used to embellish larger pieces. Old keys and locks are also extremely popular as decorative themes. I love the way that industrial items are often mixed with hearts, flowers, butterflies and insects or anything that adds a touch of femininity.

The best thing about Steampunk today is that there are no set rules. It can draw on a wide range of styles and materials which do not necessarily have to sit naturally together. Remember that Steampunk is versatile and one does not need to be a skilled jeweller to create gorgeous and unique Steampunk jewellery!

Materials

Finding and collecting materials for making Steampunk jewellery can be a hobby in itself! I have spent many pleasurable hours trawling around car boot sales, charity shops and hardware departments and have found some of my favourite pieces in places I least expected to find them! For example, when clearing out my mother's garage, I found the fabulous antique keys featured in the Antique Key Pendant project on page 36.

Over the years I have built up a collection that comes from dozens of different sources. Some materials are of indiscernible age, while others are modern representations of Victoriana. Craft stores and internet sites such as Fire Mountain Gems and Beads or Beads Unlimited don't just have the 'fun' bits but also the nuts and bolts such as the chains and jewellery findings in antique finishes that you need to construct wearable jewellery and give it that authentic look.

If you are not into taking watches and clocks apart for their gears and bits, the internet is a great source of authentic watch pieces and some sellers even list packs of parts under 'Steampunk'.

I hope you have as much fun sourcing supplies as I do!

Techniques

The Crocheted Gears Bracelet project on page 46 requires a very basic crochet technique. The step-by-step diagram below will show you how to easily achieve the single crochet technique (*UK double crochet*) that is used to make this impressive wire bracelet.

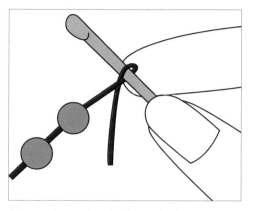

1 Insert the crochet hook into the loop in the wire.

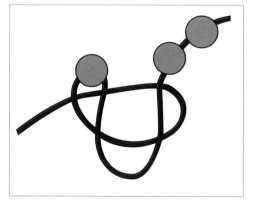

2 With the hook, reach around one of the beads and grab the wire.

3 Bring the wire through the loop and pull taut to achieve the crochet stitch.

Sea Life Lariat

Materials:

1m (1yd) of small gunmetal box chain – 2 links per 10mm (³/₈in)

4 large antique brass sea life charms – 3 x 4cm (1¼ x 1½in)

Large antique copper sea life charm – 3 x 4cm (1¼ x 1½in)

21 small antique silver-plated sea life and shell charms – 2cm (¾in)

Brass jump ring – 9mm (³/₈in)

Gunmetal jump ring – 7mm (¼in)

28 gunmetal jump rings – 5mm (³/₁₆in)

Gunmetal lobster clasp – 6 x 12mm (¼ x ½in)

Tools:

Flat nose pliers

Wire cutters

Instructions:

1 Use the wire cutters to cut the chain into two lengths of 48cm (19in) and 45cm (17¾in).

2 Use the flat nose pliers to open a small gunmetal jump ring: open the ring by finding the join and twisting. Attach the ring to the end of the 48cm (19in) chain and attach the lobster clasp to the ring as well.

3 On the opposite end of the chain, attach the large brass jump ring 9mm (³/₈in) and use this to attach a large antique brass sea life charm.

4 Attach the 7mm (¼in) gunmetal jump ring to the end of the 45cm (17¾in) chain. Then attach one of the small gunmetal jump rings to the opposite end of the same chain and use this to attach one large brass sea life charm.

5 Clip the lobster clasp to the large gunmetal jump ring on the other chain end. Open up a small gunmetal jump ring and use it to join two links from each chain strand approximately 31cm (12¼in) below the clasp. Close the jump ring.

6 Open a second small gunmetal jump ring and use it to join together another two links of chain three links below the ones joined in step 5.

Key to the Heart

As a variation on the sea life charms, use big chunky hearts and keys to create this statement piece.

7 Use another small gunmetal jump ring to attach the large copper sea life charm to the last jump ring from step 6, positioned in the centre of the lariat.

8 Use a small gunmetal jump ring to attach a small silver-plated sea life or shell charm to the top jump ring of the central join from step 5.

9 Use a small gunmetal jump ring to attach a large brass sea life charm to one side of the chain approximately 8cm (3¼in) above the top jump ring from step 5. Repeat, attaching another large brass sea life charm to the same position on the second strand of chain.

10 Use small gunmetal jump rings to attach the remaining small sea life and shell charms along the chain at regular intervals.

Corset Chain Necklace

Materials:

Approximately 75cm (29½in)
of medium gunmetal chain
– 4 links per 3cm (1¼in)

Approximately 1.5m (4ft 11in)
of spiral gunmetal chain
– 6 links per 2.5cm (1in)

Corset pendant

Pearl and chain tassel

8 jet black bicones
– 10mm (³⁄₈in)

10 ivory glass pearls
– 10mm (³⁄₈in)

16 ivory glass pearls
– 8mm (⁵⁄₁₆in)

34 gunmetal head pins

16 gunmetal jump rings
– 5mm (³⁄₁₆in)

26 gunmetal jump rings
– 7mm (¼in)

Tools:

Round nose pliers

Instructions:

1 Use the round nose pliers to open one link at the
end of the spiral chain. Remove five links and set
them aside. Repeat this process and remove a second
length of five links and set them aside.

2 Attach one of the five-link chain pieces to the
front loops at the base of the corset pendant
attaching the first link to the front left loop
on the corset and the fifth link to the front right
loop. Repeat this with the second five-link
chain and attach it to the loops at the back of the
corset pendant.

3 Open the third chain link along in both of the
five link chains and attach the pearl and chain tassel
to these links.

4 Divide the spiral gunmetal chain in half by
opening one of the links. Set one strand aside.
Open the link at one end of the chain strand and
attach to the top left of the corset pendant. Attach
the other end to the top right of the corset.

5 Take the medium gunmetal chain and open one
link at the end and attach to the top left side of
the corset. Attach the other end to the top right of
the corset.

6 Take the second strand of spiral gunmetal chain.
Open one link at the end and attach it to the top
left of the corset on the other side of medium
chain. Attach the other end to the top right of the
corset. There should be a strand of spiral chain on
either side of the medium chain.

Birdcage Multi-strand

Bird charms and blue faceted rondelles decorate this five-stranded chain with its birdcage and tassel pendant.

7 Thread all the pearls and bicone beads on to the head pins and twist the end of the pin to form a loop. Use large gunmetal jump rings to attach the large pearls and bicones to the medium chain at regular intervals.

8 Use small jump rings to attach the small pearls to both spiral chain strands at regular intervals.

Keyhole Chain Link

Materials:

Approximately 1m (1 yd) of brass chain – 3 links per 2.5cm (1in)

6 brass keyhole pieces with screw holes top and bottom – approximately 3 x 4cm (1¼ x 1½in)

6 small brass keys – approximately 3cm (1¼) long

3 larger brass keys of varying lengths – approximately 4.5–8cm (1¾ x 3¼in) long

Large brass lobster clasp

Tools:

Flat nose pliers

Instructions:

1 Use the flat nose pliers to open one link at one end of the chain. Slip on the lobster clasp and close.

2 Open the seventh link of chain below the lobster clasp. Slip off the remainder of the chain, and thread it through the top of one of the keyhole pieces and close.

3 Open the link at one end of the chain, thread it through the bottom of the keyhole piece and close.

4 Count down three links of chain, open the link, remove the remaining chain, thread the open link through the top of another keyhole piece and close.

5 Open the link at the end of the chain and thread this through the bottom of the keyhole piece from step 4 and close.

6 Repeat steps 4 and 5.

7 Count a further eleven links of chain and then open the link. Remove the remainder of the chain and thread the eleventh link through the bottom of one keyhole piece and close.

8 Open the link at the end of the chain, and thread it through the top of the keyhole piece and close.

9 Count three links of chain and open. Remove the remainder of the chain, thread the open link through the bottom of a new keyhole piece and close.

10 Repeat steps 8 and 9.

Watch Gear Chain

Create a unique chain by connecting watch parts and gears with links of chain. Some links are made up of layered gears glued together with metallic adhesive.

11 Open the link at one end of the chain, thread it through the top of the keyhole piece and close.

12 Count eight links of chain and then remove any excess chain.

13 Use one link of excess chain to attach a small brass key to the bottom of each of the six keyhole pieces.

14 Use a separate link of chain to attach each of the three medium and large brass keys to the central link (the sixth link) of chain between the two bottom keyhole pieces as shown in the image on page 12.

Winged Cog Pendant

Materials:

70cm (27½in) of large
gunmetal chain
– 2 links per 4cm (1½in)

Watch cogs piece – 4cm (1½in)

Pair of feathered wings
– 5cm (2in)

Ring of a toggle clasp
– 2.5cm (1in)

10 watch gears in varying sizes
– 1.5–2.5cm (½–1in)

3 imitation watch faces

16 faceted clear crystal
diamante flat backs
– 4mm (³/₁₆in)

2 aqua faceted crystal
diamante flat backs
– 3mm (¹/₈in)

19 gunmetal jump rings
– 9mm (³/₈in)

Gunmetal lobster clasp
– 12 x 24mm (½ x ¾in)

Jewellery adhesive

Tools:

Flat nose pliers

Instructions:

1 Glue the lower edge of the ring of the toggle clasp on to the back of the watch piece positioning it at the top. The small loop of the toggle ring should be pointing upwards at the top.

2 Glue the feathered wings to the back of the watch cog piece underneath the toggle clasp ring.

3 Glue one clear and two aqua diamante flat backs to the front of the watch cog piece.

4 Glue five clear diamante flat backs to the centre of the imitation watch faces at the '12', '3', '6' and '9' positions on the dials.

5 Attach two gunmetal jump rings to one end of the chain using flat nose pliers. Attach another two gunmetal jump rings to the first two jump rings and then attach a lobster clasp to these.

Cross Chain Link

A collection of ornate crosses decorated with diamante flatbacks and dangling from thick chain gives this piece a Gothic feel.

6 Fasten the lobster clasp to the last link on the other side of the chain. Now find the central link of chain in this circuit and use two gunmetal jump rings to attach the watch cog wing piece by the loop of its toggle clasp.

7 Attach pairs of watch gears to the chain at regular intervals using a large jump ring to hold the gears together and another large jump ring to attach the previous jump ring to the chain. Interspace these with the imitation watch faces, attaching them via a single large jump ring.

Key Charm Bracelet

Materials:

Approximately 20cm (7¾in) of brass chain
 – 4 links per 3.5cm (1⅜in)

10 brass key charms in varying shapes
  and sizes

12 amber and copper cathedral beads

12 head pins

12 brass jump rings – 5mm (³⁄₁₆in)

11 brass jump rings – 7mm (¼in)

Brass lobster clasp
 – 8 x 15mm (⁵⁄₁₆ x ⅝in)

Tools:

Flat nose pliers

Round nose pliers

Instructions:

1 Use the flat nose pliers to open one link at one end of the chain. Slip on the lobster clasp and close the link.

2 Measure the length of chain required for your wrist and remove excess links of chain by opening a link and slipping them off. Add a large jump ring to the chain end opposite the lobster clasp.

3 Thread each cathedral bead on to a head pin and use round nose pliers to form a loop with the end securing the bead.

4 Use small jump rings to attach the cathedral beads to the chain and large jump rings to attach the keys. Position the beads and keys in a random fashion along both sides of the chain links.

Hearts and Pearls

Here, the bead caps, decorative pearls and crystal rondelles add a luscious opulence to the various heart charms.

Garden Tea Party Bracelet

Materials:

Approximately 30cm (11¾in) of fine brass curb chain – 5 links per 3cm (1¼in)

Approximately 20cm (7¾in) of round brass chain – 4 links per 2cm (¾in)

2 brass chandelier earring findings with a single loop at one end and 5 loops at the other end

12 brass flower beads – 6mm (¼in)

17 flower, butterfly, dragonfly, heart and teapot charms in brass and antique silver – varying sizes 5–25mm (³/₁₆–1in)

2 brass eye pins – at least 6cm (2¼in)

28 brass jump rings – 5mm (³/₁₆in)

2 brass jump rings – 9mm (³/₈in)

Brass lobster clasp – 12 x 22mm (½ x ⅞in)

Tools:

Round nose pliers

Instructions:

1 Use the round nose pliers to attach a small jump ring to the lobster clasp. Use another small jump ring to attach the first jump ring on the clasp to the single loop end of one of the chandelier earring findings.

2 Attach a large jump ring to the single loop end of the other chandelier earring finding via another small jump ring.

3 Measure the length of chain you require between the chandelier findings. Use the pliers to remove any excess length by twisting open the chain links and slipping off the links. You should end up with three lengths of curb chain and two lengths of round chain.

4 Attach one strand of curb chain to each of the centre loops of the two chandelier findings by opening the chain link, slipping it on and closing it. Attach the remaining two curb chain strands to each of the outside loops of the chandelier findings using small jump rings.

18

Lady-Like Charm Bracelet
Miniature hand mirrors, heart lockets and sewing charms on a copper chain background reflect the pastimes of a lady in years gone by.

5 Attach the round chain to the remaining chandelier finding loops, between the curb chains, using small jump rings.

6 Take an eye pin and thread on one small flower bead. Count down from one end of the outside curb chain to the sixth link and pass the eye pin through it, then add another flower bead. Pass the eye pin through the round chain then add a third flower bead. Pass the eye pin through the middle strand of curb chain, sixth link from the end, and add a fourth flower bead. Pass the eye pin through the other strand

of round chain then add the fifth flower bead. Pass the eye pin through the last strand of curb chain, sixth link from the end, and add the final, sixth flower bead. Use the round nose pliers to form a loop at the end of the pin to close it up.

7 Repeat step 6 from the other end of the bracelet to attach another beaded eye pin.

8 Using small jump rings, attach charms to the loops at either end of the eye pins and also throughout the links of chain. Use a large jump ring for larger charms if required.

Lock & Key Bracelet

Materials:

5 brass keyhole pieces with screw holes top and
   bottom – approximately 3 x 4cm (1¼ x 1½in)

8 small keys in varying sizes and colours
   – approximately 2.5–3.5cm (1–1½in)

20 brass jump rings – 5mm ($^3/_{16}$in)

8 brass jump rings – 7mm (¼in)

Brass jump ring – 9mm ($^3/_8$in)

Brass lobster clasp – 12 x 22mm (½ x $^7/_8$in)

Tools:

Flat nose pliers

Instructions:

1 Using the flat nose pliers, attach a small jump ring to the lobster clasp. Attach this to another small jump ring and then attach this to the bottom hole of the first keyhole piece.

2 Use another small jump ring and attach the top of the first keyhole piece to two closed 7mm (¼in) jump rings, stacked one on top of the other.

3 Take another small jump ring to attach this to the bottom of a second keyhole piece, linking it to the two closed jump rings from step 2.

4 Use a small jump ring to attach the top of the second keyhole piece to two closed 7mm (¼in) jump rings.

5 Use a small jump ring to attach the side (or bottom) of the third keyhole piece to the pair of closed 7mm (¼in) jump rings from step 4.

6 Use another small jump ring to attach the side or top of the third keyhole piece to two closed 7mm (¼in) jump rings.

7 Use a small jump ring to attach the top of the fourth keyhole piece to the two closed jump rings from step 6.

8 Use a small jump ring to attach the bottom of the fourth keyhole piece to another pair of closed 7mm (¼in) jump rings.

9 Use a small jump ring to attach the top of the fifth keyhole hardware piece to the two closed jump rings from step 8.

10 Use a small jump ring to attach the large 9mm ($^3/_8$in) jump ring to the bottom of the fifth keyhole hardware piece.

11 Use small jump rings to add two keys, one on either side of all of the pairs of 7mm (¼in) jump rings between each of the keyhole pieces on the bracelet.

Watch Gears Charm Bracelet

*Watch gears and a few heart embellishments
are glued together to create layers and attached
with jump rings to form the core bracelet, with
dangling gears and a central bow.*

Watch Charm Bracelet

Materials:

Approximately 6 links of twisted wire chain
  – 3 links per 3cm (1¼in)

4 watch faces with single-hole links at top and
  bottom – 2 brass and 2 copper

21 small key charms in silver, brass and copper
  – approximately 2.5–3.5cm (1–1½in)

3 copper-coloured jump rings – 9mm (³/₈in)

2 copper-coloured jump rings – 7mm (¼in)

21 copper-coloured jump rings – 5mm (³/₁₆in)

Brass lobster clasp – 12 x 22mm (½ x ⁷/₈in)

Tools:

Flat nose pliers

Instructions:

1 Use the three 9mm (³/₈in) copper-coloured jump rings to attach the four watch faces together.

2 Use the two 7mm (¼in) jump rings to attach three links of chain to the watch face at either end of the bracelet.

3 Using the flat nose pliers, open the chain link at one end, slip on the lobster clasp and close the chain link.

4 Using the 5mm (³/₁₆in) copper jump rings, attach seven small keys to the large copper jump rings between the watch faces. Attach three to one side and four to the other side.

Guardian Angel Watch Bracelet

Pearls, crystals, hearts, flowers and guardian angels give this variation of the watch charm bracelet a romantic feel.

Victoriana Clock Charm

Materials:

Approximately ½m (19¾in) of fine gunmetal chain
– 6 links per 2cm (¾in)

Hanging marcasite watch face

2 jet black faceted peardrop glass beads
– 6 x 12mm (¼ x ½in)

2 small silver glass seed beads
– size 8

2 small antique silver bead caps
– 7 x 10mm (¼ x ⅜in)

Medium antique silver bead cap
– 10 x 12mm (⅜ x ½in)

Large antique silver bead cap
– 16 x 18mm (⅝ x ¹¹⁄₁₆in)

5 silver charms
– flowers, bows, disks

2 clear glass crystals
– 10 x 15mm (⅜ x ⅝in)

AB black bicone bead
– 6mm (¼in)

3 gunmetal head pins

1 silver eye pin

3 black eye pins

5 gunmetal jump rings
– 4mm (³⁄₁₆in)

2 gunmetal jump rings
– 7mm (¼in)

Large gunmetal lobster clasp
– 12 x 22mm (½ x ⅞in)

Tools:

Round nose pliers

Wire cutters

Instructions:

1 Use the wire cutters to cut five strands of chain of varying lengths: 5cm, 7cm, 9cm, 10cm and 11cm (2in, 2¾in, 3½in, 4in, 4¼in).

2 Open a 4mm (³⁄₁₆in) jump ring, thread on all the ends of the chain strands and then thread on to the silver eye pin.

3 Thread the silver eye pin up through the large then the medium bead cap. Use the round nose pliers to wrap the end round and form a loop to secure. Attach the lobster clasp to the loop.

4 Pass an eye pin through a black peardrop bead and thread through the small bead cap and a silver seed bead. Form a loop with the end of the pin and repeat for the other black peardrop bead.

5 Pass an eye pin through the AB black bicone bead. Use the round nose pliers to form a loop with the end of the pin and attach halfway up the 9cm (3½in) chain strand.

6 Hang the watch face from the 11cm (4½in) chain strand.

7 Attach the peardrops with bead caps to the ends of the 10cm (4in) and 7cm (2¾in) strands.

Key Timepiece Handbag Charm

Mixing metals and beads with keys adds interest to this handbag charm which has another use, namely it is also a timepiece!

8 Use the 7mm (¼in) jump rings to attach the clear glass crystals to the ends of the two remaining strands.

9 Attach the various charms to the chain strands at different intervals either by opening the chain links or by using small jump rings.

Winged Heart Cuff

Materials:

Brass openwork metal cuff

Antique silver heart and wings charm
— 2.5 x 3.5cm (1 x 1½in)

Antique silver flat back heart charms

9 antique rose pearl flat back cabochons – 5mm ($^3/_{16}$in)

6 clear faceted flat back crystals – 5mm ($^3/_{16}$in)

5 clear faceted flat back crystals – 4mm ($^3/_{16}$in)

Jewellery adhesive

Tools:

Tweezers

Instructions:

1 Use tweezers to position the heart and wings charm in the centre of the openwork metal cuff and glue into place.

2 Glue the antique silver flat back heart charms either side of the cuff at various angles.

3 Glue the rose pearl cabochons and flat back crystals on to the cuff around the hearts.

Garden Insects Lace Cuff
Flowers and insects of varying sizes are clustered and overlapping on this openwork metal cuff. Pearl cabochons and sparkling crystals add an air of opulence to this variation.

Pearl Cameo Cuff

Materials:

Base metal cuff

White on black cameo
  – 38 x 48mm (1½ x 2in)

32 ivory glass pearls – 6mm (¼in)

12 clear faceted crystal flat backs – 4mm (³/₁₆in)

22 clear faceted crystal flat backs – 3mm (⅛in)

Jewellery adhesive

Tools:

Flat nose pliers

Tweezers

Instructions:

1 Using the pliers, remove the brooch back from the cameo.

2 Glue the cameo to the centre of the cuff base.

3 Use tweezers to apply the pearls around the sides of the cameo and glue them in place – seven pearls on the first row, four pearls on the second row, three pearls on the third row and two pearls on the fourth row.

4 Fill in the gaps along the edges of the pearls with different sizes of flat back crystal.

Clockwork Cuff
Watch gears are glued around the sides of the watch cog piece and a little sparkle is added with flat back crystals.

Wirework Key Pendant

Materials:

Gold 1mm craft wire – 20cm (7¾in)

Gold 0.04mm craft wire – 2m (6ft 6in)

Brass keyhole piece – 3 x 3.5cm (1¼ x 1½in)

Brass key – 4.5cm (1¾in)

Brass jump ring – 7mm (¼in)

8 x black/gold faceted crystal rondelles
   – 4 x 6mm (⅛ x ¼in)

Small square bottle for shaping

Tools:

Round nose pliers

Wire cutters

Instructions:

1 Use a square-shaped object like a small bottle to wrap the thick wire around to get the right shape.

2 Where the wire overlaps at the ends, use the round nose pliers to make a loop.

3 Take the ends of the wire and make two or three tight wraps on either side of the loop to hold the shape. Cut off the excess wire using the wire cutters.

4 Use the thin wire to form a lattice pattern wrapping it around the thicker square frame to secure it as you go.

5 Use some thin wire to attach the keyhole piece to the sides of the thick wire square, as shown in the image, right. Wrap the ends of the thin wire round the square frame as before.

6 Thread the rondelle beads on to thin wire and attach it to the lattice around the keyhole piece.

7 Hang the key from the bottom of the pendant using the brass jump ring.

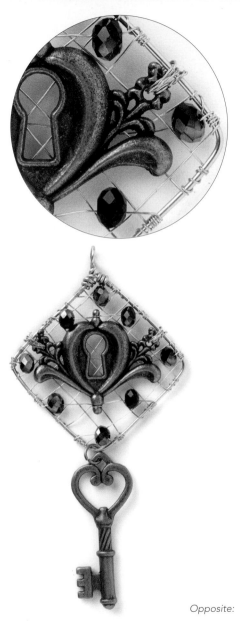

Opposite:

Pearl & Heart Cluster Pendant

Layer after layer of exquisite pearls, crystals and heart charms form this opulent pendant.

Butterfly Ring

Materials:

Openwork metal ring base
2 butterfly charms
3 pearl flat back cabochons
Jewellery adhesive

Tools:

Flat nose pliers
Cocktail stick
Tweezers

Instructions:

1 Carefully bend the larger butterfly to fit the shape of the ring base using the pliers. Glue to the centre of the ring base.

2 Use tweezers to position the smaller butterfly to the centre of the larger butterfly and glue it in place.

3 Glue the pearl cabochons to the top and sides of the butterfly using a cocktail stick to help with positioning.

Opposite:
Keyhole Ring
A diamante encrusted key hangs
from this keyhole variation.

Winged Heart Brooch

Materials:

Brooch back

Imitation compass/sextant

Heart with wings charm

2 clear crystal flat backs – 5mm ($^3/_{16}$in)

3 clear crystal flat backs – 4mm ($^1/_8$in)

Jewellery adhesive

Tools:

Cocktail stick

Tweezers

Instructions:

1 Glue the compass to the face of the brooch back.

2 Use tweezers to position the winged heart at the bottom of the compass and glue in place, as shown in the image.

3 Using the cocktail stick to help with positioning, glue the flat back crystals to the compass as a decorative embellishment.

Watch Gear Brooch

Watch gears are layered and decorated with sparkling rhinestones and a chain tassel adding an element of movement and interest to the piece.

Antique Key Pendant

Materials:

Antique skeleton key

0.08mm silver craft wire

8 small glass beads in shades of amethyst, wine and peach

Tools:

Round nose pliers

Wire cutters

Nylon jaw pliers

Instructions:

1 Cut a piece of wire about 3m (9ft 10in) long with the wire cutters. Thread beads on to the wire and form a small loop at the end to keep them from coming off.

2 Leave a tail of about 10cm (4in) of wire wrapped around the skeleton key just above the teeth of the key. Using the nylon jaw pliers, wrap the wire two or three times round the stem of the key. Position one of the beads toward the front of the key and wrap the wire tightly. Continue wrapping wire and beads all the way up to the ring head at the top of the key. Use the nylon jaw pliers to straighten the wire if it gets kinks or if you need to re-adjust any part of the wrapping.

3 Use the round nose pliers to form a loop in the wire and then continue wrapping it all the way around the ring head until you return to the stem of the key.

4 With about 5cm (2in) of wire, use the round nose pliers to form a coil to finish the end.

5 Return to the 10cm (4in) tail of wire and use the round nose pliers to form a large coil that will lay over the teeth of the key.

Golden Key
Use copper seed beads to add texture and interest to this skeleton key pendant variation.

Watch Gear Earrings

Materials:

8 watch gears

2 imitation watch face charms
  – 18mm (¾in)

2 imitation watch face charms
  – 12mm (½in)

2 brass chains of 5 links each
  – 4 links per 3.5cm (1¾in)

10 clear flat back crystals – 3mm (⅛in)

2 fish hook ear wires

Jewellery adhesive

Tools:

Flat nose pliers

Cocktail stick

Tweezers

Instructions:

1 Glue one crystal to the centre of the larger imitation watch face charm and one on each of the watch gears using a cocktail stick to help position the crystals.

2 Take one of the five-link brass chain pieces and open one of the chain links at the end. Attach a large imitation watch face charm. Close up the chain link.

3 Using the pliers, open the next chain link along and slip on one watch gear. Close up the chain link.

4 Open the next chain link along and slip on one watch gear on the opposite side from the previous one and close the chain link.

5 Open the next chain link along and slip on one watch gear on the opposite side from the previous one. Close up the chain link.

6 Open the last chain link. Slip on the small imitation watch face charm, then attach the fish hook ear wire and then another watch gear. Close up the chain link.

7 Repeat for the second earring.

38

Flowers and Bow Earrings
Bow earrings with flat back crystals and garden insect charms make a softer variation.

Key Cuff Links

Materials:
2 cuff link blanks
2 antique silver keyhole pieces
2 brass keys
Jewellery adhesive

Tools:
Tweezers

Instructions:
1 Glue the keyhole pieces to the cuff link blanks. Allow to dry.

2 Glue the keys on to the top of the keyhole pieces, at an angle, using tweezers to help with positioning. Allow to dry.

40

Nautical Cuff Links
Antique sextants are mounted on watch gears to create the nautical flavour of these cuff links.

Secret Garden Bracelet

Materials:

Approximately 2m (6ft 6in) of brass round chain – 4 links per 2cm (¾in)

1m (1yd) of clear stretch cord – 1mm

4 ivory glass pearls – 6mm (¼in)

4 clear faceted crystal rondelles – 6 x 8mm (¼ x ⅜in)

8 antiqued silver bead caps (4 each of 2 different designs)

8 silver ball head pins

Approximately 13 flower, butterfly and bee charms (use 2 where charms are single sided)

20 brass jump rings – 7mm (¼in)

8 brass jump rings – 4mm (⅛in)

1 large spare bead

Clear nail varnish

Tools:

Round nose pliers

Wire cutters

Darning needle

Instructions:

1 To create the bead units, thread each pearl on to a silver ball head pin then pass through a bead cap and form a loop with the end of the pin. Next, thread each crystal rondelle on to a silver ball head pin then pass through one of the alternative bead cap designs and form a loop with the pin.

2 For the charms, use round nose pliers to open and attach a 7mm (¼in) jump ring to each one. Where the charms are only one sided, place two charms back to back on one jump ring.

3 Count the links of chain and divide the number of chain links by the number of charms you are using: this tells you where to place beads or charms. Don't count the bead units; they will be added later.

4 Thread the darning needle with stretch cord, making it double ply. Thread on a large spare bead bigger than the chain link and stitch around the bead a second time to secure. (This will keep the end of the thread from passing thought the links and the beads once they are threaded.)

Watch & Gear Chain Link
Gears, clock faces and watch hands on a gunmetal chain make an industrial, edgy variation.

5 Use the needle to weave back and forth through the chain links, stopping to pass through the jump ring of a charm at regular intervals. For small links of chain, I find it best to weave back and forth through every other link of chain. Note: Sometimes I use more than one jump ring if I want the charm to hang down further so it can be seen. Simply attach another jump ring to the jump ring on the bead.

6 When you get to the other end of chain and have added all the charms, remove the spare bead and tie the four strands of stretch cord together in an overhand knot. Seal with clear nail varnish and allow to dry before cutting away excess cord using wire cutters.

7 Attach the bead units to the chain links wherever you like, using small jump rings.

Watch Cog Ring

Materials:

Inside of an old broken watch
– 15 x 18mm (½ x ¾in)

Small gears from an old broken watch

Pair of antique silver wings – 1.5 x 2cm (⅝ x ¾in)

Crystal diamante flat backs
– 3mm and 4mm (⅛in and ³⁄₁₆in)

Ring base

Jewellery adhesive

Tools:

Cocktail stick

Tweezers

Instructions:

1 Using tweezers to position them, glue gears to the inside of the watch piece.

2 Glue the inside of the watch piece to the ring base.

3 Glue the wings to either side of the watch.

4 Glue diamante flat backs on to the gears inside the watch, using a cocktail stick to help with positioning.

Chandelier Finding Ring
A chandelier earring finding decorated with a mother of pearl heart and small crystal rhinestones creates an elegant ring reminiscent of another century.

Crocheted Gears Bracelet

Materials:

Approximately 6m (19ft 8in) of 0.04mm gold-coloured craft wire

25 gold glass pearls – 6mm (¼in)

12 grey pearls – 6mm (¼in)

22 grey glass pearls – 8mm (³⁄₈in)

11 small and medium watch gears in silver, gold and gunmetal –15–20mm (6–7¾in)

3 small imitation clock faces – 12mm (½in)

2 antiqued gold-coloured bead caps – 10mm (½in)

2 gold-coloured jump rings – 7mm (¼in)

Large gold lobster clasp – 12 x 22mm (½ x ¾in)

Tools:

Flat nose pliers

Wire cutters

Crochet hook – 3.75mm (US F/5)

Instructions:

1 Use the wire cutters to cut four lengths of wire, each 1.5m (4ft 11in) long.

2 On one wire, thread the gold pearls and use the pliers to form a loose loop at the end to keep the beads from slipping off. Form another loop about 15cm (6in) from the end of the wire, large enough to insert the crochet hook.

3 Insert the crochet hook into the loop and slide a bead up next to the hook. With the crochet hook, reach around the bead and grab the wire, carefully bringing it down past the bead and through the loop. See the step-by-step diagrams on page 7.

4 Repeat the crochet process from step 3 to make more stitches until you have the right length of pearls for your bracelet. Add or remove pearls as required. Set aside when finished.

5 Take another length of wire and thread on the large grey glass pearls and form a loop at the end to keep them from falling off. Form another loop about 15cm (6in) from the end of the wire. Repeat the crochet process from step 3, except this time crochet one pearl, then crochet one stich without a pearl, then another stitch with a pearl. Repeat this until you have a length of large grey glass pearls approximately 5cm (2in) longer than the strand of gold pearls.

6 Take a third length of wire and thread on the small grey pearls. Form a loop at the end to keep them from falling off. Form a loop about 15cm (6in) from the end of the wire. Repeat the crochet process from step 3, except this time crochet a pearl, then crochet two stiches without a pearl, then crochet another stitch with a pearl. Repeat until you have a length of small grey pearls approximately 5cm (2in) longer than the strand of gold pearls.

7 Take a final length of wire, thread on the watch gears and imitation clock faces and form a loop to keep them from falling off. Form a loop about 15cm (6in) from the end of the wire. Repeat the crochet process from step 3, except this time crochet a gear or watch face, then crochet two stiches without a gear, then another crochet stitch with a gear. Repeat until you have a length of gears approximately 5cm (2in) longer than the strand of gold.

8 Take the gold pearl strand and the large grey pearl strand and twist them together until they are both the same size. Then twist the strand of small grey pearls around this double strand.

10 Twist in the strand of gears so that they are positioned all around the pearls of the first three strands.

11 Bend the ends of any two of the wire strands and fold them back into the bracelet weaving them into the other wires. Be sure to cut off any excess and ensure the ends do not poke out.

12 Now, taking the ends of the two remaining wire strands, pass them through a large grey pearl then the small gold bead cap. Form a loop and wrap the excess wire around the base until you are sure the loop is secure. Repeat for the other side of the bracelet.

13 Use a gold jump ring to add the lobster clasp to one end of the bracelet and add the other gold jump ring to the other side of the bracelet.

Acknowledgements

The author would like to acknowledge the following suppliers who provided many of the materials used in this book.

Beads Unlimited
www.beadsunlimited.co.uk

HobbyCraft
www.hobbycraft.co.uk

Crystal Parade
www.crystalavenue.co.uk

Solid Oak
www.solidoakllc.com

Fire Mountain Gems and Beads
www.firemountaingems.com

Viking Loom
www.vikingloom.co.uk